50
NEW
PRAYERS
FROM THE
IONA COMMUNITY

50 NEW PRAYERS FROM THE IONA COMMUNITY

NEIL PAYNTER

www.**ionabooks**.com

Prayers © the individual contributors
Compilation © 2012 Neil Paynter
First published 2012 by
Wild Goose Publications, Fourth Floor, Savoy House,
140 Sauchiehall Street, Glasgow G2 3DH, UK,
the publishing division of the Iona Community. Scottish Charity No. SC003794.
Limited Company Reg. No. SC096243.

ISBN 978-1-84952-216-8

The publishers gratefully acknowledge the support of the Drummond Trust,
3 Pitt Terrace, Stirling FK8 2EY in producing this book.

Neil Paynter has asserted his right in accordance with the Copyright, Designs and Patents Act, 1988, to be identified as the author of this compilation and the individual contributors have asserted their right to be identified as authors of their contributions.
A catalogue record for this book is available from the British Library.

Overseas distribution
Australia: Willow Connection Pty Ltd, Unit 4A, 3–9 Kenneth Road, Manly Vale, NSW 2093
New Zealand: Pleroma, Higginson Street, Otane 4170, Central Hawkes Bay
Canada: Bayard Distribution, 10 Lower Spadina Ave., Suite 400, Toronto, Ontario M5V 2Z

Printed by Bell & Bain, Thornliebank, Glasgow

CONTENTS

INTRODUCTION

This book includes prayers from folk of all ages – from 93-year-old Ian Fraser, a former Executive Secretary of the World Council of Churches, who has spent much of his Spirit-led life travelling the world visiting basic Christian communities, to a prayer from a young woman, Fiona Barker, a member of the Iona Community's Resident Group on Iona, who (compared to Ian) is more at the beginning of her life journey.

It also includes prayers from people around the globe – from Glasgow to Cincinnati, from Malawi to Alaska ...

Former Leader of the Iona Community Kathy Galloway has written: *'The Community is both a worldwide movement – with members and groups everywhere from Malawi to Michigan, from Cumbria to Cuba and from Perth, Scotland to Perth, Australia – and a movement rooted in local realities.'*

I always feel inspired and energised when I think about this: Folk doing what they are called to do in their own community – everything from collecting door to door for Christian Aid to protesting non-violently at Faslane nuclear submarine base. 'We all have our gifts,' wrote Saint Paul. 'We are all members of the Body.' We are all sparks of the Light, I think.

And so I think of some of the members, associates and friends of the Community in this little book:

Israel Nelson, a retired substance abuse counsellor in Alaska, campaigning for decent, humane housing for a vulnerable friend and his family; June Walker working at the grassroots, promoting permaculture in Malawi; John Harvey hosting meetings and helping to enable those participating in the Poverty Truth Commission; Katy Owen volunteering at a foot clinic for the homeless in Glasgow; Reinhild Traitler working at the European Project for Interreligious Learning, EPIL, in Zurich; Chris Polhill welcoming pilgrims to her and her husband's beautiful and challenging Reflection Gardens in Cannock Wood; Ian Fraser still 'hammering out theology at white heat in the fire of experience', and digging his vegetable garden at his but-and-ben in Fife; politician Ewan Aitken working for peace and justice in the City of Edinburgh; scholar Rosemary Power leading prayer walks in County Clare ... I think too of the sister communities in this book, like the Open Door Community in America, welcoming the homeless of Atlanta into 910 Ponce De Leon Avenue; visiting sisters and brothers in prison.

I think of the work of this community of wonderful, committed people (and others) – all of them in their own particular, passionate, dogged way helping to build Christ's Kingdom; work sustained by a daily discipline of prayer.

50 New Prayers offers prayers that might be used in a daily discipline, many on the concerns of the Iona Community – poverty and economic justice, interfaith dialogue, welcome and hospitality, church renewal, peacemaking …

They are new prayers, in that they haven't appeared in Wild Goose books before and are not published in books elsewhere that I know of, and there are some newer 'voices'.

This is not in any way a definitive collection of 'new prayers from the Community'. I simply chose the prayers from a collection of seeds I reached down into and have scattered.

I've avoided dividing up these prayers into sections or themes or days. There's a flow. If you're looking for a prayer for a service it shouldn't be hard to find one.

I hope that these prayers find their way into your church – and I hope that you carry this wee book with you out into the world. I know I'll carry it with me, on the train or bus to work: to connect with the still small voice in the midst of the busyness and babble. On demos and marches: to root myself firmly in the Word.

And I think of it as counter-cultural: carrying a pocketbook of prayers around with you in your coat or handbag or rucksack at a time in the West when there is an attack, by the Conservative Party and others, on the poor, on asylum seekers and immigrants – on Christ in the stranger – and in intellectual circles, on God.

There are prayers here for the renewal of global and local community, and for recharging the battery of your mobile phone:

'Either He is the Lord of everything or He is Lord of nothing,' wrote George MacLeod, founder of the Iona Community.

Thanks to Yvonne Morland who helped to collect the prayers in this book, and thanks to her for her own sensitive, poetic writing.

May this little book help to bring and to kindle light.

Neil Paynter, Lent 2012,
Biggar, Scotland

May prayer feed your actions
and may your actions
feed the world ...

50 NEW PRAYERS FROM THE IONA COMMUNITY

A SIMPLE PRAYER

God,
I have a simple prayer for the Church.
I pray that one day soon
I will be part of a church that when we pray for the poor,
we will pray for 'us' and not 'them'.
I pray for a Church that will not only have the courage
to work for the poor,
to struggle with the poor
but will also be of the poor.
And I pray that one day
there will be no poor people in the Church
because there will be no poverty.
And I pray to you,
the God of miracles,
the God of the rich,
the God of the poor.
Amen

*Martin Johnstone, Church of Scotland's Priority Areas Secretary;
Chief Executive, Faith in Community Scotland*

http://faithincommunityscotland.org

'YOU ALWAYS HAVE THE POOR WITH YOU' (MARK 14:7)

Our trouble,
Jesus,
is that 'the poor' are seldom 'with us'.
Too often,
we keep people who live in poverty at arm's length:
in sink estates,
in 'developing' countries,
and think of them as victims,
or a burden,
or worse.

By your solidarity with the outcast and the rejected
you honoured their humanity
and released their potential.
Forgive us our arrogance
and our stupidity;
open our hands and our hearts
to receive the gifts they bring;
and show us how to work together
so that the curse of poverty
may be outlawed from the earth.

John Harvey, Poverty Truth Commission

www.povertytruthcommission.org

'BLESSED ARE YOU POOR' (LUKE 6:20)

Blessed – how?
There's never enough money –
every pay day is 'pay away' day –
and the Benefits system
makes me feel dirty and ashamed.
The bankers get bonuses
for plunging the whole country into debt;
me, I get blamed, and threatened with the law.
I'm tired and I'm angry
and the last thing I feel is 'blessed'.

So, Jesus,
if you really mean it,
if this blessing you talk about
is for here, and not just for eternity,
then this is my prayer:

Change the culture of this country –
upset not just the tables but the spirits
of the men with money and power –
give me the words and the wisdom
to speak my truth to them,
and give them the patience and the pity
to listen;

then maybe, just maybe,
we'll all get a blessing in the end.

John Harvey, Poverty Truth Commission

BY NAME

Made in your image,
every single one.
Knit together,
every single one.
Called into being,
every single one.

No matter what the headline says.
No matter what the state of my purse says.
No matter what my postcode says.
No matter what my accent says.
Every single one.

Called into being,
called by my name.

No matter where I shop.
No matter who I sit next to.
No matter what the label.
No matter.

God of the poor.
God of the rich.
God of the struggling somewhere in between.
Rise with us in the morning and dare us to dream.
Turn our heads with your vision of justice and joy.
May we work together with hope as our guide.

May we greet all your children by name alone.
Amen

Elaine Downie, Facilitator for the Poverty Truth Commission

IN YOUR NAME

Heavenly Father, we thank you for your love and generosity, given in abundance: so no one should go hungry.

We pray for people living in poverty, judged and written off, that they may have a place at the table.

We pray for a world that has become materialistic: guide us to recognise that people are more valuable than objects, especially for the sake of those living in poverty.

Please help those who close their hands and eyes to the plight of people in poverty, that they may open their hearts and show compassion to those less fortunate than themselves and be led into action.

Heavenly Father, you created us as loving and caring people. Send your Holy Spirit to guide us to embrace all who are living in poverty; help us to stand alongside them and support them to have their God-given right to a decent life with the opportunity to contribute.

We ask this in your name. Amen

Tricia McConalogue, Projects Coordinator, Bridging the Gap; Co-chair, Poverty Truth Commission

www.bridging-the-gap.org/aboutus.html

SIFTING AND SORTING

Lord
here, in my head and my heart,
the kaleidoscopic fragments of this day –
  sights and sounds
  words and thoughts
  snatches of conversation
  moments of silence
  energy and weariness
all whirl together
scintillating, elusive and distracting …

Help me to turn them gently
until the pieces
settle
and the patterns become clear.

Pat Bennett, England

O ETERNAL CHANCELLOR OF LOVE

Behind the facts and figures,
you wait,
watching the business
and the busyness
of the earth.

You see clearly
how our compulsive desires
overwhelm our best intentions:
how we sell out the best that is in us
and pay lip service to your will.

We presume
that all we have is by automatic right,
that all we have is due to our own industry.

We collaborate, unconsciously,
in building and sustaining a society
that enslaves the spirit,
that impoverishes human bodies,
that displaces being with having.

O Eternal Chancellor of love,
through the centuries of accumulating interest,
our multiple accounts have gone into arrears;

our outstanding loans remain toxic;
our borrowings in months and pounds
have been unwisely and selfishly spent,
when they should have been credited
to the statement sheet
of the world
and all people,
and not just a few.

May we, with you,
re-audit our assets of time and money,
and recalculate our budgets
so that they become redeeming, redistributional and just.
May deep gratitude
replace our unthinking expenditure;
and may deeper compassion
more regularly repay the excessive capital of your love.
We pray this in Jesus' name
Amen

Wild Goose Resource Group

FROM YOUR UNENDING BOUNTY

Creator of the cosmos,
forgive us our wickedness in allowing concepts such as
'commodity futures' and
'sub-prime mortgage lending'
become a part of our culture.
May we learn from the faiths of others
the concepts of 'economics as if people mattered',
of 'giving to the poor and lending without interest',
of 'sharing the surplus'
from your unending bounty
so we are no longer burdened by having
more than we need.

June Walker, Malawi

LUKE 4

So many necessary international agreements
have been signed by our governments –
we should expect life to be thriving for all people –
for the whole precious creation.

Patient and loving God,
don't let us settle for empty words,
because human rights –
gender justice, cultural rights, economic justice,
all of this and more –
really are what you taught us to work for
and to follow faithfully.

How was it then that Jesus began his ministry according to Luke 4?:

'The Spirit of the Lord is upon me,
because he has anointed me
to bring good news to the poor.
He has sent me to proclaim
release to the captives
and recovery of sight to the blind,
to let the oppressed go free,
to proclaim the year of the Lord's favour.'

I presume he meant it seriously –

so why do so many who think that what Jesus said is important
not take human rights seriously?

There are great women and men who *do* take this seriously,
who commit their life to it;
and lots of them feel the church is not the place for them –
they are rejected, persecuted,
their own rights are trampled on …

God, that must make you feel cross –
I know it makes many of us cross.

God, keep us on track,
working together even more so
when things aren't working out as they should;
but they will, won't they, God?

Robert Jordan, Argentina

GOD OF ALL LIFE

God of all life

in the places of power
let the voices of the voiceless be heard.

In the places of wealth
let the plight of the poor be understood.

In the places of plenty
let those living in poverty be remembered.

In the places of decisions
let your kingdom be the watchword.
Amen

Ewan Aitken, Scotland

IN GOD'S ACCOUNT

In God's account
no person, creature
is more precious
than any other part
of the wonderful creation
God made right at the start.

The way I speak,
the way I look,
the colour of my skin
is perhaps the reason
you keep me out.
But God will keep me in.

Lord, teach us to be gracious:
to pronounce mercy on what we fear,
to be willing to be proved wrong,
to value what you hold most dear.

Yvonne Morland, Scotland

PRAYER OF THE PARTNER'S BELOVED

O loveliest of lovers,
sacred partner to all and to each!

Your love takes me beyond myself:
I become what you desire.

Your intimate knowledge attends my needs,
and I respond with gladness.

Your forgiveness renders me fully alive
when I am cold and frigid.

Your warm embrace enfolds me:
never let us separate.

Our mutual love spills into the world.
Co-creators, co-redeemers, co-habiters
together – two becoming one.

Blessed are you, my sacred partner,
and loveliest of lovers!

Sharon Francis, England

HOLD US IN YOUR MERCY

Loving God be there:

When we cannot be ourselves for fear of others' hate.
When we cannot love ourselves for self-loathing is too great.
When everything we say is construed another way.
When it's clear from 'our' communities that they wish we'd go away.

Keep us speaking of our love, which is faithful to your call.
Keep us demonstrating that sexuality is not our all.

Hold us in your mercy through all our earthly days.
Till we come home to you, rejoicing in your praise.

Yvonne Morland, Scotland

GOD OF SURPRISES

God of surprises,
who chose not the mighty but the vulnerable
to be the vehicle of your salvation.
Give us the courage of Mary to say 'yes'
to your vision of a world made whole,
that we may labour with creation
to give birth to justice and new life.

Annabel Shilson-Thomas/CAFOD

LORD OF THE MORNING

Lord of the morning,
you come to us in sunshine and in shower.
Unobtrusive, you call us into life once again.
We long for your love to enfold us,
your Spirit to refresh us and renew us,
your gentle presence to guide and protect us.
In return we offer you our grateful thanks –
ourselves just as we are.

Like Bartimaeus, we sit by the roadside
listening and waiting for your approach.
Like him we want to leave the past behind and move on.
And so we offer you all that hurts and harms and demeans us
and the ways we hurt and harm and demean other people.

Heal our offences,
redeem our weakness
and enable us to forgive and be forgiven.

Lord, we delight in your presence;
we feel your grace around and within us
making us whole,
encouraging us, urging us on.
We are glad to be part of this community of faith.
May your Spirit show us the way that leads to life.
Amen

Katy Owen, Scotland

LORD OF THE WALL

We are all guilty.
We build barriers to hide what we do not want to see.
We draw lines through other people's hearts.
We trample with our feet what others hold dear.
We defend ourselves by dividing others from their rights.

Jesus,
in the land where your feet were tired,
where you carried the burden for the oppressor,
where you broke the chains of the prisoner
and set our hearts free,
may those who plant olives harvest them,
may those who build houses live in them;
as we honour the graves of our neighbours
may peace flourish till the moon fails.

May we learn to see welcome in the eyes of the people we fear.

Rosemary Power, Ireland

BLESSED ARE THE PEACEMAKERS

Jesus, peacemakers go into situations of distress and hatred.
They try to bring change.
Often they are at a loss.
You blessed the peacemakers.
You promised to help them.
But you did not talk about success;
you told us to go and work for peace …

And if we don't see any result
are we still blessed and sons and daughters of God?
Is the path to peace a walk that will never end?

Jesus, son of God, you yourself failed,
you died as a political criminal –
but your message is still alive!

Jesus, help all peacemakers to continue in hopeless places;
empower us not to give up hope.
Give us today the courage to walk the long road to peace,
to take small steps in the wilderness of war, torture, injustice
and keep the flame of peace burning.

*Elisabeth Christa Miescher, volunteer with the Ecumenical Accompanier
Programme in Palestine and Israel, www.eappi.org*

A BLESSING FOR THE PEOPLE OF THE BOOK

The blessing of the God of Sarah and Abraham
the blessing of the God of Hagar and Ishmael

the blessing of the God Jesus loved so much
that he called him 'Father'
the blessing of the God who spoke to Mohammed
through the angel Gabriel

the blessing of God's Spirit that is eternally at work in all of creation
that moves between us and within us
and enables us to do the work of love

the blessing of God be with us
now
here
evermore!
Amen

Reinhild Traitler, Switzerland

OVER MANY NEW JERUSALEMS

Long have you wept, O Lord,
over many new Jerusalems
where many of your faithful people
wage war instead of peace.

Bring a new word to the world, O God,
both angry and ringing with mercy,
that, long deaf, we may hear once again
the voices of those we oppress.

So that justice may roll down like a river,
the captives be released from their bonds,
our hearts be turned once again,
to love tenderly, walk humbly with you.

Yvonne Morland, Scotland

OUR FIRST ALLEGIANCE

Lord Jesus,
you have taught us a golden rule:
to do for others as we would have them do for us.
A golden rule that is taught throughout religions of the world.
And yet the world is still divided unfairly,
race against race, culture against culture, creed against creed.
And while every faith preaches peace and justice
we go on sowing seeds of suspicion, seeds of prejudice,
against those who are different from ourselves.
God forgive us!
Challenge our sense of belonging
until our first allegiance is to the human race itself.
For your broken body still longs for healing,
Lord Jesus.

Brian Woodcock, England

GOD OF PEACE

God of peace,
in the wilderness of conflict
let us hear your voice
and be challenged to repent.
Fill us with your holy rage
that we may join your protest
and proclaim the injustice of war.
Embolden us with the Gospel of hope
that we may oppose oppression
and proclaim liberation.
Amen

Annabel Shilson-Thomas/CAFOD

PRAYER FOR RECHARGING THE MOBILE

As I recharge my mobile battery
may God recharge my soul:
the current of God's love
flowing through me
healing, restoring, renewing …

As the ions return to their source,
I to Jesus return.
Plug me into your kin-dom,
your way for life –
loving, forgiving, truthful.

As I sit waiting by my mobile
connect my life to you.
God's Spirit in my thoughts.
Help me listen
to your love, your prompting,
deep within.

Chris Polhill, England

YOU

You

greater than all we can think of
smaller than all we can imagine

you

farther than the universe and beyond
nearer than the secret of our hearts

you

breath of being
before us and behind us

you

force of life
above us and beneath us

you

speaking in many human tongues
whispering in the depth of our souls

we come into your presence to praise you
because you are

and we are
through you and together with
you
now and for ever.

Reinhild Traitler, Switzerland

DENALI, THE GREAT ONE

Creator God,
who calls us into being
and gives us Mother earth as our dwelling place,
remind us please –
and remind us often –
that earth is our only true home.

When the fireweed blooms,
show us in its beauty
how we must cultivate clean waterways
for the salmon to come home and spawn,
and provide us with food.

Teach us the wisdom of the Inuit people
who use all of Brother Whale
when he is harvested from the Bering Sea
so that nothing is wasted.
Remind us to give something to the walrus
so that he will come again
and provide us with abundance.

You sustain us in the Great Land and we are truly grateful.

You are Denali, the Great One,
and from You comes the gift of our life.
With Jesus, our brother, we give You praise.
Amen

Israel Nelson, Alaska

LET US LEARN

Let us learn from the indigenous people,
whom we have so wronged,
who did not fit our development plans,
whom we have swept aside
as we divided the planet between us
and plundered it.

Let us learn that the land is sacred.
Let us learn to walk lightly on the earth.
Let us learn our need of forest and wilderness.
Let us learn the natural rhythms.
Let us learn our need of rites of passage.
Let us learn, and not patronise.
Let us learn, and ask forgiveness.
For they have not gone away.
Not yet.
Not quite.
Let us learn,
while there is still time.

Brian Woodcock, England

WHERE THERE SEEMS NO END

Where there seems no end to hunger and poverty,
or to the fear of landmines and AIDS,
enter the brokenness of the people and their land
with your healing love, O God.
But also enter, and make visible,
their rich cultures, their deep faith,
their work for peace,
and their joyous celebration of life.

Prayer from Iona Abbey

A PRAYER FROM THE PILSDON COMMUNITY

This beautiful and very powerful prayer is used at Sunday Eucharist at the Pilsdon Community in England, one of the Iona Community's sister communities.

We break this bread for those who love God,
for those who follow the path of the Buddha,
and worship the God of the Hindus;
for our sisters and brothers in Islam,
and for the Jewish people from whom we come.
We pray that one day we may be as one.

We break this bread for the great green earth;
we call to mind the forests, fields and flowers
which we are destroying,
that one day, with the original blessing,
God's creation will be restored.

We break this bread for those who have no bread,
the starving, the homeless and the refugees,
that one day this planet may be a home for everyone.

We break this bread for the broken parts of ourselves,
the wounded child in all of us, for our broken relationships,
that one day we may glimpse the wholeness that is of Christ.

Donald Reeves

The Pilsdon Community seeks to provide an environment where people can rebuild their lives after experiencing a crisis, whether sudden or progressive. Since 1958, the Pilsdon Community have been offering a refuge to people in crisis, those working through depression, alcoholism, addiction, divorce or bereavement. The Community also welcomes people who wish to find a time to reflect on their lives before making a change in direction, or just want time out to live as part of a community (from the Pilsdon Community website: www.pilsdon.org.uk).

IN EVERY SACRED SPACE

Heart of God:

on mountaintops crowned with mist,
and in museums filled with wonder;

in tents pitched by singing brooks
and in theatres filled with laughing children;

in every
sacred space
and in all
the ordinary neighbourhoods,
you are with us,

listening to us,
hearing us,
answering us,
and we do not lose
heart.

Thom Shuman, USA

PRAYER FOR LOCAL COMMUNITY

We pray for the places where we live:
our own local communities
of people who never chose one another
but are nonetheless interconnected
in a delicate balance of public and private,
of services and shops, schools and streets,
of events and concerns.
We pray for the public-spirited, for local activists,
for noisy neighbours
and for those who hide in lonely rooms.
These people, these activities,
they are your gift to us.
And we are your gift to them.
Thank you, living God!

Brian Woodcock, England

FROM THE GRASSROOTS

Lord God of all,
who out of nothing
created this universe and launched it on its way
in nebulae and starry clusters;
who opened the eyes of the prophet to see
life-giving possibilities in a valley of dry bones;
who raised Jesus Christ from the dead;
give us the insight,
when situations seem without hope,
to stand before you as did Ezekiel,
empty-handed and expectant,
to affirm what you,
the source of life,
may do which is beyond our power.

Wherever this world husbands but
'a little life with dried tubers', *
we give thanks that,
from the grassroots,
you call people to emerge,
as would seed to bear fruit;
who in small communities and house churches

turn to you to find a trustworthy promise of new life for the world,
who set out, in community,
to know you better and take your Way,
growing in faith and helping others to become mature –
that transformed life may mark the world's course.

We rejoice in you,
God the Lord,
who,
out of nothing,
summons into being the church to be like light and salt,
giving life meaning and flavour.
Amen

Ian M. Fraser, Scotland

* T.S. Eliot, from 'The Wasteland'

IN OUR DISABILITY

Creator God, you see where we can't see.
You hear where we can't hear.
You speak where we can't speak.
You move where we can't move.
You are able where we are disabled.
Share with us your ability, and bless us in our disability.

Christ our Brother, you were blindfolded:
be with us in our blindness.
You communicated by sign language:
be with us in our deafness.
You were paralysed on the cross:
be with us in our immobility.
You were dismissed as being crazy:
be with us in our learning difficulty.
You were disabled when you were treated as rubbish:
rejected Christ, scarred Christ, risen Christ,
be with us and for us.
Take us as we are,
and make us what you want us to be.

John and Shirley Davies, Wales

CHURCH-BORN-FROM-BELOW

'Waters shall break forth in the wilderness, and streams in the desert.'
Isaiah 35:6

Lord God, we acknowledge that you are the Great Doer;
at our best we but respond to your initiatives.
You know us through and through
and our lives are fulfilled when they honour your promise for them.

We bless you that in our day we see the prophecy of Isaiah fulfilled.
Where the church seems to be in decline,
the 'church-born-from-below' appears in small communities
and house churches
in which people seek together to discern and live your Way.
So we know that you, the Father,
are unremitting in your love for your creation;
that you, the Son, have resurrection power;
that you, the Spirit, bring life where death reigned.

So we bless you that we live hopefully because you are with us,
and will never leave yourself without a witness.
To you be the glory for ever and ever.
Amen

Ian M. Fraser, Scotland

THE ADVENTURE OF COMMUNITY
A PRAYER FROM IONA

God who walks with us the adventure of community,
remind us of your constant presence.

When we are full
give us the strength to bring light to others.

When we are empty
comfort and renew us.

When we need challenge
teach and stretch us.

And when we need rest
provide a stopping place on the way.

Fiona Barker, Resident Group member on Iona

WITHOUT HUMAN MASTERS

Lord Jesus Christ, you said:
'Where two or three are gathered in my name
I am there among them.'
We know that that gives you your unique place –
the centre which is life-giving, which we can affirm by grace.
We know that it is to you and no other
that all authority is given in heaven and on earth.
Yet we confess that your church is continually tempted
to raise other authorities to positions which may distract
from your unique centrality.

So we give thanks for the sign provided
by small Christian communities
that to gather in your name
is to relate to the only authority that matters;
that since such communities *'are self-convened*
before the Living-Word-in-Christ,
without human masters' *
they tell us to seek you alone
as we find our way through life.
You will be there, with us, we know
and we give you all the glory.
Amen

Ian M. Fraser, Scotland

* An often-quoted basic Christian communities' understanding of 'church'.

'MY' YOUNG PEOPLE

Eight nieces and nephews
aged twenty-six to twenty-one
each growing forth in the world
in ways I can see but not know.
Inherited feuds in the family
keep us from each other's company:

A girl piper who practises hospitality.
A cool guy with a passion for Celtic!
An artist who likes to go fishing.
A young mother of one little boy.
A sensitive American student.
A gymnast who took her own life.
A tall, spare, athletic sportsman.
A young soldier, now in Iraq.

God, bless and have mercy on them all.
Keep them free from harm.

Yvonne Morland, Scotland

WITH THREADS OF LOVE

New voices
new stories
fresh ideas
fresh perspectives
startling songs –
awesome adventures!

Each day is a sea to be surfed,
a mountain to be biked,
a rock to be scaled,
an injustice to be challenged.

Our deepest longing for all young people
is that their life is interwoven with the threads of love,
of joy,
of creativity
and of justice.

And that those who have lived longer
see God in these threads
and listen and learn
and give thanks.

Prayer from Iona Abbey

WORDS

(i)

With words:
we scribble and scrawl
we wrestle and pray
we wound and shame
we touch and heal
we praise and prophesy

May our words be grounded in your Word, O God.

(ii)

Words can jump and fly
Words can touch the sky
Words can ease your sorrow
So you're hopeful for tomorrow

In the depths of night
Words are out of sight
Except within our hearts
Where all our prayer starts

Words about our God
Words about our Lord

Words about the holy
Words about the lowly

With the Spirit's Word
Though it seems absurd
Silent though we pray
Our hearts shout glad 'Hurray!'

Yvonne Morland, Scotland

YOUR FACE IN THE FACE OF EACH OF US

Holy Creator God,
only now are we beginning to understand how You made us,
and that we are really all related.
What an irony that we are all descended
from the same African ancestor!
Yet we have evolved to be many colours,
many shapes,
many sizes,
speaking many languages.
And You love us all,
each and every one,
in a way unique to each one.

How dare we put up dividing walls of concrete and hostility
to wall out
or wall in
those who are different!

However gently,
however forcefully You must do it,
we need You to show us how to value each other
regardless of gender
or preference
or colour
or language.

Your Law is Love.
Help us to honour each one's right to uniqueness.
Show us again that there are no limits to the love You have for us:
so we cannot limit our love for each other.
It really is true that to love another is to touch Your face.
Brother Jesus saw Your face in the face of each one of us.

Help us to see his face in the face of each other
so that we can bring about peace in Your world.
Amen

Israel Nelson, Alaska

WIDE ENOUGH

God of aliens and strangers:
make the doors of our homes
wide enough
so all find a home.

God of the near and far off:
make our hearts
wide enough
so all might find a friend.

God of saints and sinners:
open our arms
wide enough
so all –
the politician, the homeless man,
the neighbour, the guest,
the child, the widow –
may be wrapped in your grace.

Thom Shuman, USA

THE CORINTHIAN SIGN

Father, Son and Holy Spirit,
we confess that we celebrate Pentecost
yet fail to express in our practice the reality
that the fire of the Spirit descended on everyone present,
conferring gifts for building up the church for ministry in the world;

that while we give thanks for those who are deservedly prominent,
who sustain and enlarge our vision,
we too often neglect those gifts distributed among your people
which need to be identified, matured and brought into play.

We give thanks for basic Christian communities,
house churches and Family Groups
where different gifts are shared
and even the shy have their silence and thoughtfulness
made a creative contribution.

Save us from being like a ship laden with fruit
whose crew and passengers starve.
Hold before us the Corinthian sign:

'Every time you come together
each one has a hymn,
a lesson, a revelation,
a tongue or its interpretation.
Bring everything to bear
for building up the church.' (1 Cor 14:26)

Make us teachable before that word, we pray.
We ask it in Jesus Christ's name.
Amen

Ian M. Fraser, Scotland

A CANDLE OF HOPE IN A DIVIDED WORLD

Thank you, Jesus, for your astonishing gifts to us:
your multifaceted teaching, in parable and paradox;
your all-embracing love that encompassed
such an unlikely mix of people
and invited them to get along.

Thank you for your great array of contradictory witnesses;
and for your explosive Spirit
that pitched them out into the world
before they had agreed upon a single version of the story.
Thank you, Jesus, for your church of many colours.

Give us the humility to welcome your gifts,
and all the traditions that bring them to us.
Help us to delight in difference,
to listen and learn
and blur the boundaries
and work together for you.
Make us a broad church;
a broad and generous church;
a candle of hope in a divided world.

Brian Woodcock, England

PLACES OF REST AND REFRESHMENT

Places of rest and refreshment are found
sometimes where we least expect them.
In the midst of the chaos of life
when we're too burdened to lift our heads.

God may throw a stone in our path
over which we stumble upon new vision:
O God, help us to see these stones
as objects of blessing, not of cursing.

Guide our steps through the doors
where a welcome and shared bread awaits,
and help us provide such refreshment
for others you place in our lives.

Yvonne Morland, Scotland

FROM OUR OWN FRAGILE RESOURCE

Lord Jesus Christ,
as you drew from your own spittle and from the dust of the ground
all that you needed to heal a man born blind,
so from you and from our own fragile resource
do we draw all that we need
to offer healing to a world which does not know which way to turn.

Graeme Brown, Orkney

THIS DAY

Forgive us, Jesus,
when we cling to the familiar;
block the possibilities;
insist on the old ways.
Forgive the fears
that bind us to the past

Teach us instead
to trust the Spirit's leading;
risk new expressions;
offer *this* day in worship.
Knowing your love
is there on every path.

Chris Polhill, England

INCARNATE GOD

Incarnate God:
let us be the voice of the silenced.
Let us be the passion of the subdued.
Let us be the shoulder for the struggling.
Let us be the light for the lost.

Let us be your challenge for change,
true to your call for justice to flow like a river
and hope to spill over like a waterfall
in word and sign and symbol and song
in our lives.

Amen

Ewan Aitken, Scotland

WINTER PRAYER

Lord of the lights that fire the winter sky,
Creator of the ice that bridges rivers;
who brings spring when birds return to nest;
Spirit of summer torrents, lover of mountain corries,
let us lay our nests by your altars.

God of the long rest of winter,
of the green suddenness of summer,
God of those who live with extremity and create equality.

May we learn to value each person as your own;
and in our little windows to the dark
open our eyes to a blade of grass and a star.

Rosemary Power

('A blade of grass and a star' is a quote from the Icelandic writer Halldór Laxness)

ON HOLY GROUND

Go gently, my friends:
feel the good earth
beneath your feet,
celebrate the rising of the sun,
listen to the birds at dawn,
walk gently under
the silent stars,
knowing you are on holy ground
held in love –
in the wonder of God's creation.

Peter Millar, Scotland

PILGRIM PEOPLE

Walking together
Singing psalms
Breaking bread
Pouring wine
Arguing fiercely
Speaking truth lovingly
Dancing on the earth
Spinning with the stars …

O God, we are your followers
going where you lead us,
whether we have wanted to
or known what we must do.

With an adventurous spirit
may we always step lightly,
with your yoke upon us,
on our journey home to you.

Yvonne Morland, Scotland

REMIND US

God in whose love we are made,
when bread is before us
remind us of the hungry.

When our key is in our door
remind us of those who have no home.

When we enjoy the opportunities of money in our pockets
remind us of those who only know poverty.

When the laughter of friendship fills our hearing
remind us of those who know only loneliness.

When the love of our family keeps us safe
remind us of those whose family was the place of their pain.

When we wonder what it is we can do,
remind us that you said:

'Whenever you feed the hungry, clothe the naked,
welcome the stranger, visit the prisoner,
you do it to me.'

Remind us

and lead us to do
as you call us to do.

Amen

Ewan Aitken, Scotland

OPEN DOOR COMMUNITY JESUS PRAYER

The Open Door Community, in Atlanta, Georgia, is one of the Iona Community's sister communities.

Our Beloved Friend
Outside the Domination System
May your Holy Name be honoured
by the way we live our lives.
Your Beloved Community come.

Guide us to:
Walk your walk
Talk your talk
Sit your silence
Inside the courtroom, on the streets, in the jail houses
as they are on the margins of resistance.

Give us this day everything we need.
Forgive us our wrongs
as we forgive those who have wronged us.
Do not bring us to hard testing,
but keep us safe from the Evil One.
For Thine is:

the Beloved Community,
the power and the glory,
for ever and ever.
Amen

Open Door Community, Atlanta, Georgia

The Open Door Community is a residential community in the Catholic Worker tradition (we're sometimes called a Protestant Catholic Worker House). We seek to dismantle racism, sexism and heterosexism, abolish the death penalty, and proclaim the Beloved Community through loving relationships with some of the most neglected and outcast of God's children: the homeless and our sisters and brothers who are in prison.

We serve breakfasts and soup-kitchen lunches, provide showers and changes of clothes, staff a free medical clinic, conduct worship services and meetings for the clarification of thought, and provide a prison ministry, including monthly trips for families to visit loved ones at the Hardwick Prisons in central Georgia. We also advocate on behalf of the oppressed, homeless and prisoners through non-violent protests, grassroots organising and the publication of our monthly newspaper, Hospitality.

(From the Open Door Community website:
http://www.opendoorcommunity.org)

NEW
PRAYERS
IONA COMMUNITY

FROM THE

THOUGHTS ON PRAYER: FROM A SCRAPBOOK

Collected quotes from a 'scrapbook' on prayer … (Ed.)

To begin and end the day in prayer is to wrap the day in sanctity – all events and encounters within that time are then encompassed in God's care.

Annie Heppenstall, Wild Goose Chase (Wild Goose Publications)

Prayer may be expressed in work. In Ecclesiasticus 38, the writer looks at the upholding of daily life by basic workers – ploughman, engravers, smiths, potters – and concludes that *'their daily work is their prayer'* – the thought and expertise invested in it make it not just a labour, not even just a labour of love, but an offering. The will of God is seen to be fulfilled by the way in which their offering moves life forward: *'Without them a city would have no inhabitants … they sustain the fabric of the world.'*

I asked a joiner who supplied two doors for me, whose craftsmanship elsewhere in the village I had admired, whether he would rather get a large payment for some rushed and rather substandard work or inadequate payment for work on which he had lavished craftsmanship and extra time. He did not want to answer such a theoretical question. But it was clear from his few stumbling words that he would be fixed on doing the job well, letting nothing come in his way. I am pretty sure he would never have thought of that commitment as having prayer in it.

Ian M. Fraser, A Storehouse of Kingdom Things
(Wild Goose Publications)

To be a Christian without prayer is no more possible than to be alive without breathing.

Martin Luther King

I cannot pray for a young person in prison if I do not look for ways to relieve the boredom of unemployment, the pressure of advertising, the board and lodgings legislation that keeps him on the move, and the lure of drugs, that have combined to destroy his liberty. I cannot pray for people who are poor in my community, or for that matter for people who are hungry, oppressed and poor anywhere else in the world, if I do not challenge the way that my country's government spends its resources.

I say I cannot pray. What I mean is that I cannot pray for the healing of others with integrity without also acting on my prayers. If I am blind to the sources of injustice around me, and divorce the needs of an individual from the pain of a whole community, my prayers for healing are non-sense and bear no resemblance to the good news of the gospel.

Ruth Burgess, Praying for the Dawn
(Wild Goose Publications)

So many people think that it is only holy and pious sorts of folk that pray, and that it is unnatural. But that is just nonsense. If you believe in God, it is most unnatural not to pray.

But what is even more important to remember is that we have to act as well as pray, if our prayers are going to be answered as God wants them to be answered. For instance, King Hezekiah prayed that Jerusalem should have a better water supply, but it did not come by magic. Hezekiah had, as we say, to take his jacket off, roll up his sleeves, and dig the tunnel.

Roger Gray, an early member of the Iona Community

Follow the light you have
and pray for more light.

George MacLeod

Prayer is no monopoly of those who are religiously inclined. It is a constituent element of human existence. And mountains may give praise to God simply by existing, as they are … To rejoice in a slave people who escaped from Egypt, 'the slave-pen', the mountains 'skip like rams'. The psalmist does not see praise of God confined to human beings, though we have responsibility to articulate it:

Praise the Lord from the earth …
… Mountains and all hills,
fruit trees and all cedars,
wild animals and all cattle,
creeping things and flying birds …

Recourse to prayer is woven into the fabric of the universe.

Ian M. Fraser, A Storehouse of Kingdom Things
(Wild Goose Publications)

Prayer does not change God but it changes the one who prays.

Kierkegaard

In September 1940, when the incendiary bombs were raining on London, it looked as if the rebuilding might have to be stopped because of lack of timber. Then the deck cargo of a Swedish ship carrying wood from Canada had to be jettisoned. The timber floated all the way to Mull, directly opposite Iona – all the right length.

'Whenever I pray,' said the beleaguered Dr MacLeod, 'I find that the coincidences multiply.'

From George MacLeod: A Biography, Ron Ferguson (ed)
(Wild Goose Publications)

Question: 'What is prayer to you?'
Answer:

> '… Prayer is working in my garden.
> Prayer is sitting in my garden.
> Prayer is sharing food
> from my garden.
> Does that make sense?'

From a conversation with a friend

Call on God but row away from the rocks.

Indian proverb

God speaks in the silence. Listening is the beginning of prayer.

Mother Teresa

I often think that this is the most important of all, and that is the prayer of thanks. There is simply no limit to the things we have to say thank you for. There is the sun and moon, the sunshine and rain, the sea and rivers, the birds and animals, in fact the whole of nature. Then there are our parents, our friends, our health and strength.

One of the things I am always thanking God for is that I am alive at this time of history. I think this is a marvellous age and I am grateful just to be alive and able to help in the tremendous jobs that need to be done.

Roger Gray, an early member of the Iona Community

If the only prayer you ever said was 'Thank you', you would have said all the prayers.

Meister Eckhart

The greatest prayer is patience.

The Buddha

What difference do our prayers make? This isn't a question just for people who go to church. Prayer is not the preserve of any one group. There is something naturally human about praying, especially in times of difficulty and need – out of our concern for others and for ourselves. What are we expecting to happen when we pray? Is it that whoever or whatever we are praying to will bring about some miraculous laser beam intervention?

Prayer is essentially an act of solidarity – an expression of our own need, a yearning for a better world, a commitment to belonging together. We pray not only with our lips but with our lives. And every little act of justice, caring and generosity counts.

Norman Shanks, a member of the Iona Community

Dietrich Bonhoeffer talks about the need for 'holy worldly' people – followers of Jesus who live in the world but who are also sustained by an arcane, or secret, discipline of prayer. 'Contemplation' or 'action' are false alternatives. Both are involved in the Christian lifestyle. A person who prays deeply will be driven to act against injustice. Similarly, a Christian who is engaged in the problems of the world will be driven to prayer. Contemplation need not be escapism, a turning one's back on the world which God loves. Prayer is at the heart of a genuine Christian radicalism – one which truly gets to the root of the matter.

Ron Ferguson, Chasing the Wild Goose (Wild Goose Publications)

Souls without prayer are like bodies, palsied and lame, having hands and feet they cannot use.

St Teresa of Avila

Is it not the essence of prayer – to see the One who is always near, and who is constantly inviting us, in gentle compassion, to come back to our inheritance as a human being made in the divine image?

Peter Millar

God responds to human situations where actual prayer is not clearly involved. So oppressed were the Hebrew people in Egypt under their task-masters that they seemed only to groan and cry out, without shaping their words into prayers. It was enough. God hears cries, and answers cries as well as prayers.

Ian M. Fraser, A Storehouse of Kingdom Things
(Wild Goose Publications)

Prayer is really good fun, can become good fun, and the future of our Church is going to be funny until we can write that sentence.

George MacLeod

I have so much to do that I shall spend the first three hours in prayer.

Martin Luther

And if a relationship with God is to count rather than be a casual affair, there have to be deliberate decisions as regards the use of time, money and prayer which will consolidate the relationship and affirm its worth.

John Bell, Thinking Out Loud (Wild Goose Publications)

Perhaps the task, our need in communion with God and in reflective prayer, is to sit in the observation car at the rear of the train. There, we can see where we have come from, see this and that fall into its proper place, find a perspective, and believe and know that if our God has guided us thus far, we can trust him enough to take us on to the next stage.

Tom Gordon, A Need for Living (Wild Goose Publications)

Some of us need reminding from time to time that prayer is not something we do when we curl up in some religious corner. Prayer belongs to the nature of God. God's Spirit prays within us, prays within all our faculties and not just those with religious labels attached.

The letter to the Romans testifies to God's Spirit praying, groaning in the whole created universe as in the pangs of birth. It is a continual groaning within the travail both of Palestinian and Israeli communities, within the long chill winter in Afghanistan, within the forgotten earthquake communities of Gujarat, within the communities of Bosnia and Kosovo now returning to our screens through the trial of Milosovitch in the Hague.

Our shared testimony is to God's Spirit brooding within the world's chaos, creating, forming, wooing and calling into being.

Donald Eadie

Spirituality is the place where prayer and politics meet.

Kate McIlhagga, member of the Iona Community

The ego is a veil between humans and God.

Rumi

So prayer for me is an auditing, hauling the boulders of self-absorption, fear and prejudice away from where they sit midstream, blocking the flow of life. And it's an opening ourselves up to the reality, the gift, the struggles and suffering of others, being present to and with them insofar as we are able, even if it's only one day of the month with the help of the Rogues' Gallery (a book of photographs of the Iona Community members). And prayer, particularly intercessory prayer, is a making visible.

The Japanese-American theologian Kosuke Koyama writes: *Grace cannot function in a world of invisibility. Yet in our world, the rulers try to make invisible the alien, the orphan, the hungry and thirsty, the sick and imprisoned. This is violence. Their bodies must remain visible. There is a connection between invisibility and violence. People, because of the image of God they embody, must remain seen.*[1]

We make visible what is hidden, to ourselves first, and look for where our prayer will be earthed.

And then there are these flowing moments of prayer which are gratitude, appreciation, mindfulness: *The turn of a leaf in morning sun and the catch in our throat drives us to our knees and into prayer.*[2]

Kathy Galloway, Living the Rule: The Rule of the Iona Community (Wild Goose Publications)

Essentially, prayer is about listening to God – that God who inhabits the deepest places of our being.

Peter Millar, Our Hearts Still Sing (Wild Goose Publications)

How many are the individuals who rightly decide to engage in personal prayer, but wrongly take care that the answer to prayer – the power of God coming into them – is not allowed to have issue through them and out into the world. And how soon do such protest that 'the machine is not working'.

God, in fact, is answering as surely as an electric current is entering a man even though he be not earthed: but His power is simply returning to its source. The man does not feel it because he is insulated.

Conviction of power, in the life of a congregation as of an individual, depends on being earthed. We must have constant outside contact to keep alive.

One description of the Incarnation is that God deigned to become earthed. And a correct description of the Church on earth is that it is the extension of the Incarnation. But God became incarnate not to be lost in the earth, but that the world, through Him, might be saved.

George MacLeod

Prayers go up and blessings come down.

Yiddish proverb

Prayer is where the action is.

John Wesley

There are evenings when our prayer life is refreshing: but, analysed, they turn out to be the times when the pressures have been so weighty that you have simply had to go with them to God. But this is precisely the recovery of the knife-edge. The religious moment flowers from the practical …

In the true life of prayer we are forever on the knife-edge. We move in the light and shadow of Him who is born Son of God and Son of Man. Manifestly there is a new prayer life demanded: not stationary times with God, but living, flowing times when, by His Spirit, we are exercised in unravelling the mystery of that apex of majesty which is His humanity.

George MacLeod

If the heart wanders, bring it back to the point quite gently and replace it tenderly in its Master's presence. Even if you did nothing during the whole of your hour but bring your heart back and place it again in our Lord's presence, though it went away every time you brought it back, your hour will be very well employed.

St Francis de Sales

What debilitates our prayer life, I suggest, is our presupposition that the pressures of life are on one side while God is on some other side. With this presupposition, when evening comes with an ending to our pressures, we are apt to go eagerly to God – disconcertingly to find a vacuum. We seek to fill the vacuum with 'spiritual thoughts'. The more we try, the more desperate does the situation become: till in effect we say that we are not really the praying type.

George MacLeod

The fruit and the purpose of prayer is to be oned with God in all things.

Julian of Norwich

It is better in prayer to have a heart without words than words without a heart.

Gandhi

Our prayers must be about earthly things, even as the answers are about heavenly things. Jesus Christ is the interpreter both of God and of history: in Him is the Atonement. And those who are His must be, simultaneously, very mystical and very material.

The reality of worship and prayer is not found in abstraction from life but in engagement with the kingdoms of this world, in light of the promise that they will become God's Kingdom. It is the whole world which is to be brought in and spread out before God when the people assemble, as Hezekiah spread out his letter. It is sin in all the dimensions in which it thwarts God's loving purpose, small-scale and large-scale, which is to be confessed. It is the whole field of the world which is to be irrigated by forgiveness, offered up with hope and expectation, entered into by a company prepared to present their bodies as 'a living sacrifice'.

Ian M. Fraser, The Way Ahead (Wild Goose Publications)

Properly understood and applied, prayer is the most potent instrument of action.

Gandhi

Pray without ceasing …

1 Thessalonians 5:17

Notes:

1. From an address given by Kosuke Koyama at the 8th General Assembly of the WCC, Harare, Zimbabwe, 1998

2. From the poem 'Paradox' by Yvonne Morland, from *Pushing the Boat Out: New Poetry*, ed. Kathy Galloway, Wild Goose Publications, 1995

SOURCES AND ACKNOWLEDGEMENTS

'O Eternal Chancellor of Love' – From Holy City liturgy, Nov 2008 ©
WGRG, Iona Community, Glasgow G2 3DH, Scotland.

WILD GOOSE PUBLICATIONS IS THE PUBLISHING HOUSE OF THE IONA COMMUNITY, WHICH IS:

- An ecumenical movement of men and women from different walks of life and different traditions in the Christian church

- Committed to the gospel of Jesus Christ, and to following where that leads, even into the unknown

- Engaged together, and with people of goodwill across the world, in acting, reflecting and praying for justice, peace and the integrity of creation

- Convinced that the inclusive community it seeks must be embodied in the community it practises

Together with its staff, the community is responsible for:

- The islands residential centres of Iona Abbey, the MacLeod Centre on Iona, and Camas Adventure Centre on the Ross of Mull

and in Glasgow:

- The administration of the Community

- Work with young people

- A publishing house, Wild Goose Publications

- Its association in the revitalising of worship with the Wild Goose Resource Group

The Iona Community was founded in Glasgow in 1938 by George MacLeod, minister, visionary and prophetic witness for peace, in the context of the poverty and despair of the Depression. Its original task of rebuilding the monastic ruins of Iona Abbey became a sign of hopeful rebuilding of community in Scotland and beyond. Today, it consists of about 280 Members, mostly in Britain, and 1500 Associate Members, with 1400 Friends worldwide. Together and apart, the community 'follows the light it has, and prays for more light'.

For information on the Iona Community contact:
The Iona Community, Fourth Floor, Savoy House,
140 Sauchiehall Street, Glasgow G2 3DH, UK.
Phone: 0141 332 6343
e-mail: admin@iona.org.uk; web: www.iona.org.uk

For enquiries about visiting Iona, please contact:
Iona Abbey, Isle of Iona, Argyll PA76 6SN, UK.
Phone: 01681 700404

For books, CDs & digital downloads published by Wild Goose Publications: www.ionabooks.com

Wild Goose Publications, the publishing house of the Iona Community established in the Celtic Christian tradition of Saint Columba, produces books, e-books, CDs and digital downloads on:

- holistic spirituality
- social justice
- political and peace issues
- healing
- innovative approaches to worship
- song in worship, including the work of the Wild Goose Resource Group
- material for meditation and reflection

For more information, please contact us at:

Wild Goose Publications
Fourth Floor, Savoy House
140 Sauchiehall Street,
Glasgow G2 3DH, UK

Tel. +44 (0)141 332 6292
Fax +44 (0)141 332 1090
e-mail: admin@ionabooks.com

or visit our website at
www.ionabooks.com
for details of all our products and online sales